THE STATUE OF LIBERTY

by Susan Rose Simms

Cody Koala
An Imprint of Pop!
popbooksonline.com

abdopublishing.com
Published by Pop!, a division of ABDO, PO Box 398166, Minneapolis, Minnesota 55439.

Printed in the United States of America, North Mankato, Minnesota

032018
092018

THIS BOOK CONTAINS RECYCLED MATERIALS

Cover Photo: Shutterstock Images
Interior Photos: Shutterstock Images, 1, 6, 9, 13 (top), 13 (bottom left), 13 (bottom right), 14, 16, 17, 19, 20, 21; iStockphoto, 5; Red Line Editorial, 10–11

Editor: Meg Gaertner
Series Designer: Laura Mitchell

Library of Congress Control Number: 2017963477

Publisher's Cataloging-in-Publication Data
Names: Simms, Susan Rose, author.
Title: The statue of liberty / by Susan Rose Simms.
Description: Minneapolis, Minnesota : Pop!, 2019. | Series: US symbols | Includes online resources and index.
Identifiers: ISBN 9781532160486 (lib.bdg.) | ISBN 9781532161605 (ebook) |
Subjects: LCSH: Statue of Liberty (New York, N.Y.)--Juvenile literature. | National monuments--Juvenile literature. | Emblems, National--Juvenile literature.
Classification: DDC 974.71--dc23

Hello! My name is

Cody Koala

Pop open this book and you'll find QR codes like this one, loaded with information, so you can learn even more!

Scan this code* and others like it while you read, or visit the website below to make this book pop.

popbooksonline.com/the-statue-of-liberty

*Scanning QR codes requires a web-enabled smart device with a QR code reader app and a camera.

Table of Contents

Chapter 1

America's Lady

The stately **statue** of a woman rises high above an island near New York. She is the Statue of **Liberty**. People come from all over the world to see her.

Watch a video here!

At first Lady Liberty honored the friendship between America and France. Now she stands for peace and liberty for all.

The statue's full name is Liberty Enlightening the World.

Chapter 2

The History of Liberty

Lady Liberty now stands on Liberty Island. But she was first built in France. It took nine years to build her out of **copper**.

Lady Liberty was brown at first, but the copper turned green over time.

Frédéric Bartholdi, sculptor

Complete an activity here!

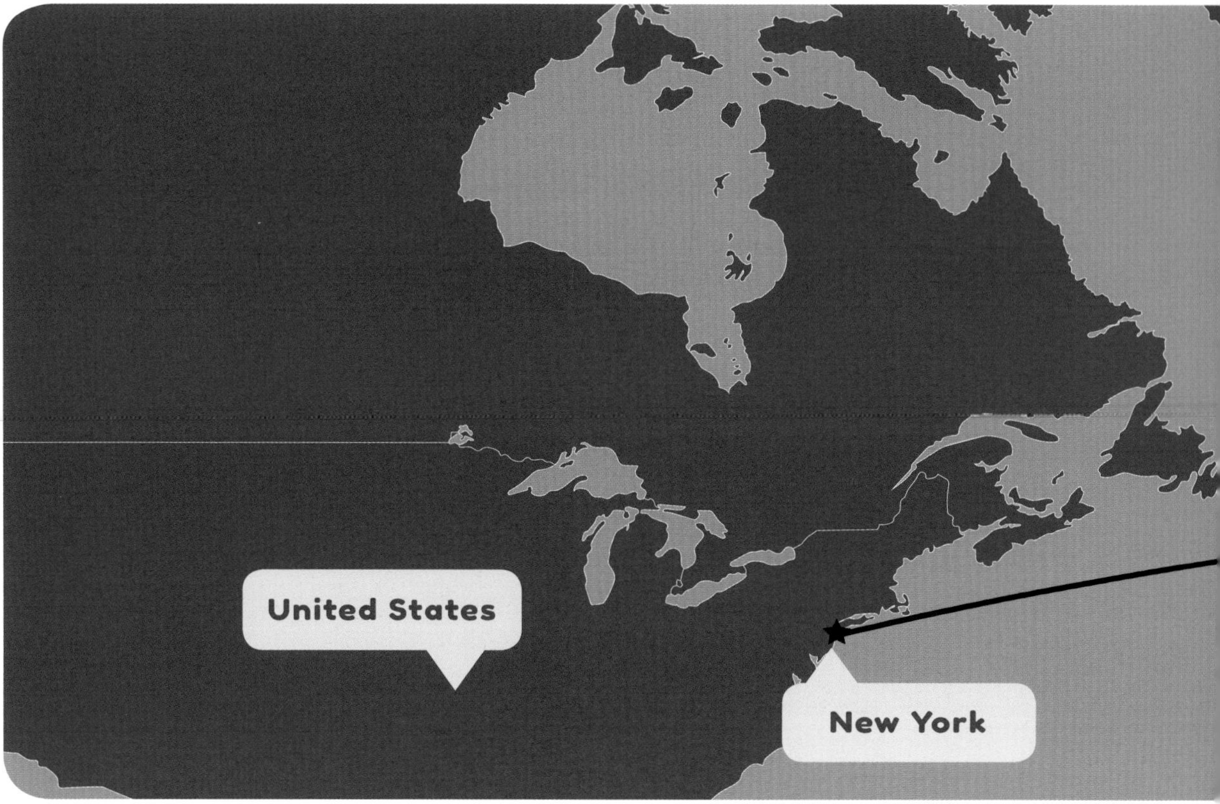

She was brought to America on a ship. She came in many pieces.

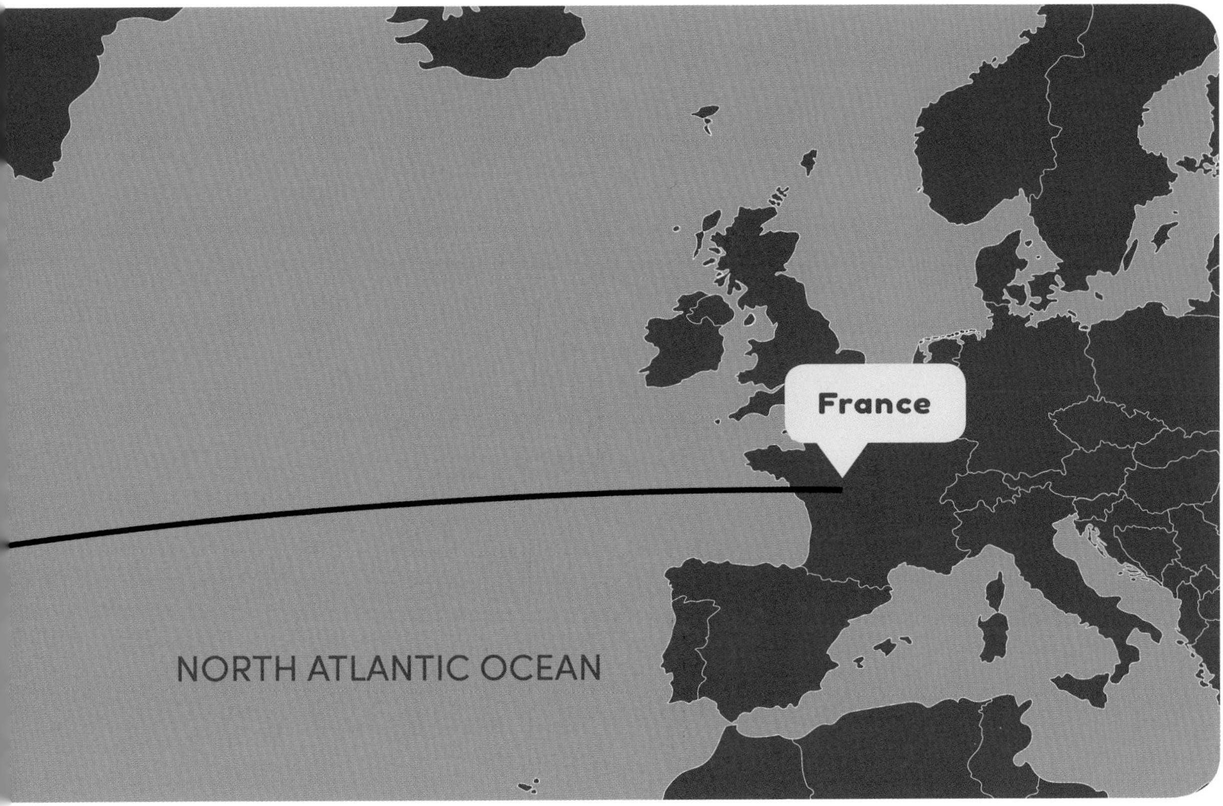

It took four months to put her together again. She was finished in 1886.

Chapter 3

Liberty Stands Tall

From ground to tip, Lady Liberty is as tall as a building with 22 floors. She wears a crown with seven points.

Learn more here!

The points stand for the seven seas and the seven **continents**.

People can climb 354 steps to her crown. They can stand inside her crown and look out many windows.

Lady Liberty holds a **torch** and a **tablet**. The torch shines light on the path

to liberty. The tablet has the date America became free written on it.

Chapter 4

Liberty for All

Emma Lazarus wrote a **poem** about the statue. The poem welcomes people who move to America from other countries. People come for a new start and a better life.

Learn more here!

For many people, the Statue of Liberty is a sign of hope. The statue

says they can be free in America. It says everyone is welcome here.

Making Connections

Text-to-Self

It took nine years to build the statue. Think of something you've built. How long did it take you? How did you feel when it was completed?

Text-to-Text

Have you read about any other symbols of the United States? What did you learn about them?

Text-to-World

The statue is a symbol because it stands for something else. What other symbols do you see in your life? What do they stand for?

Glossary

continent – one of the seven large land masses on Earth.

copper – a reddish-brown metal that turns green over time.

liberty – freedom, the right to do as you like.

poem – writing that is done in short lines.

statue – a figure of a person or animal made out of metal, stone, or wood.

tablet – a block of stone with writing on it.

torch – a flaming light that can be carried in the hand.

Index

Online Resources

popbooksonline.com

Thanks for reading this Cody Koala book!

Scan this code* and others like it in this book, or visit the website below to make this book pop!

popbooksonline.com/the-statue-of-liberty

*Scanning QR codes requires a web-enabled smart device with a QR code reader app and a camera.